I0821843

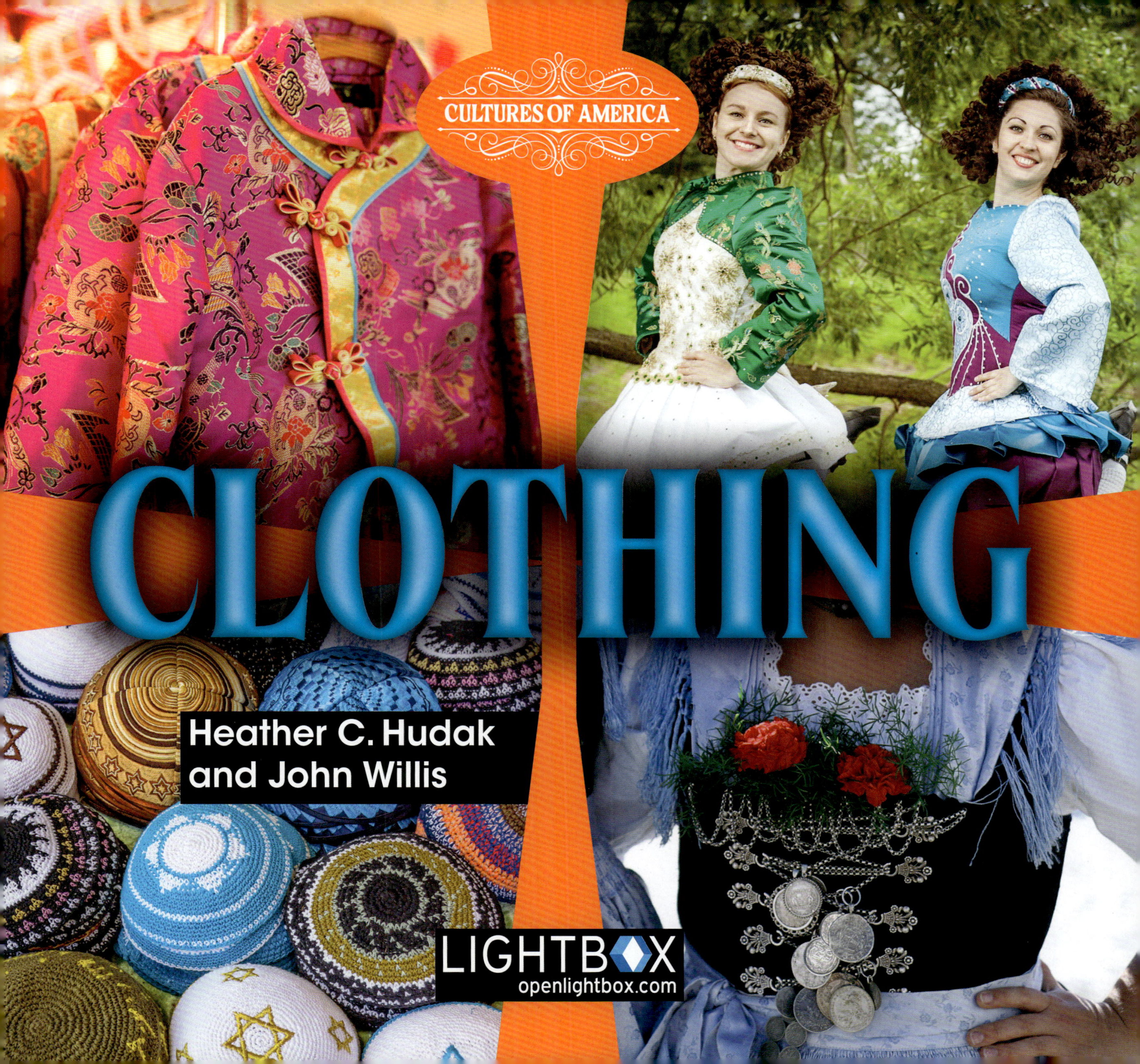
CULTURES OF AMERICA
CLOTHING
Heather C. Hudak
and John Willis
LIGHTBOX
openlightbox.com

LIGHTBOX

Go to **www.openlightbox.com** and enter this book's unique code.

ACCESS CODE

LBXM4855

Lightbox is an all-inclusive digital solution for the teaching and learning of curriculum topics in an original, groundbreaking way. Lightbox is based on National Curriculum Standards.

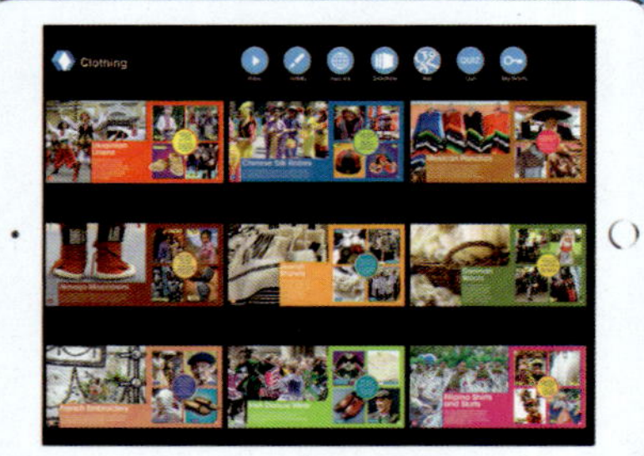

OPTIMIZED FOR

- ✓ TABLETS
- ✓ WHITEBOARDS
- ✓ COMPUTERS
- ✓ AND MUCH MORE!

STANDARD FEATURES OF LIGHTBOX

- **AUDIO** High-quality narration using text-to-speech system
- **VIDEOS** Embedded high-definition video clips
- **ACTIVITIES** Printable PDFs that can be emailed and graded
- **WEBLINKS** Curated links to external, child-safe resources
- **SLIDESHOWS** Pictorial overviews of key concepts
- **INTERACTIVE MAPS** Interactive maps and aerial satellite imagery
- **QUIZZES** Ten multiple choice questions that are automatically graded and emailed for teacher assessment
- **KEY WORDS** Matching key concepts to their definitions

SUPPLEMENTARY RESOURCES

- **SHARE** Share titles within your Learning Management System (LMS) or Library Circulation System
- **CURRICULUM** Find national and state curriculum correlations
- **CITATION** Create bibliographical references following the Chicago Manual of Style

VIDEOS

WEBLINKS

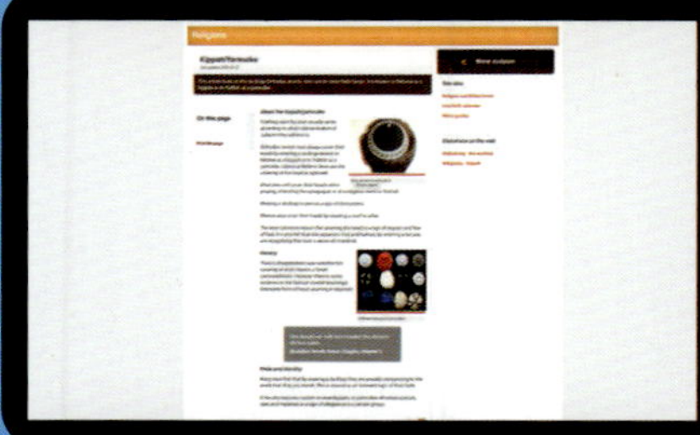

SLIDESHOWS

QUIZZES

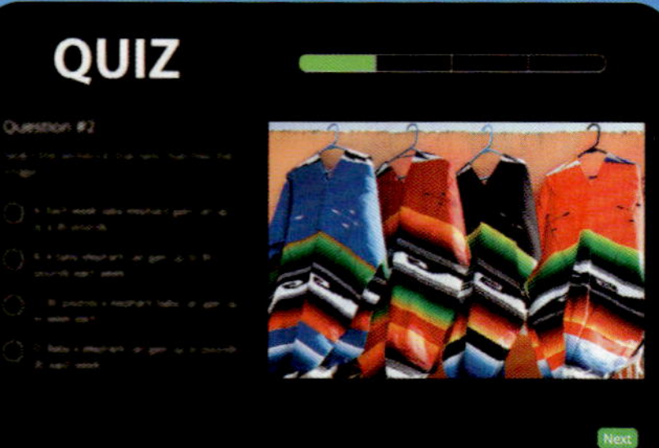

This title is part of our Lightbox digital subscription

Lightbox Grades K–5 Subscription
ISBN 978-1-5105-5712-3

Access hundreds of Lightbox titles with our digital subscription.
Sign up for a **FREE** subscription trial at **www.openlightbox.com/trial**

CLOTHING

CONTENTS

Ukrainian Linens

Ukrainian clothing is made from a handwoven linen called polotno. Polotno is often decorated with embroidery. There are more than 100 types of Ukrainian embroidery stitches. A shirt is called a sorochka. Young girls wear a sorochka with no belt. Young women wear a sorochka with a belt instead.

Ukrainians use embroidery to decorate their clothing.

On what types of clothing do you use embroidery stitches?

Chinese Silk Robes

The Chinese traditionally wear silk robes or tunics. Women wear long robes with a belt. Men wear robes that come to their knees. Sometimes, they wear a jacket over the robe. If it is cold, they may wear pants as well. A yi fu is a short jacket. Ku are pants. A qun is a skirt. Mao is a hat.

Scarf

Cheongsam

Chinese traditional robes are made from silk.

What kind of material is used to make your traditional clothes?

Mao

Xie

Mexican Ponchos

Ponchos are sleeveless coverings. They are made from rectangle-shaped cloth pieces with a hole for the head. Ponchos have been worn by people in Central America and South America for hundreds of years. In Mexico, ponchos are traditionally made from cotton or wool. Today, many people wear ponchos to keep dry or for fashion.

Ponchos are a very old design but are still worn today.

Why do you think they are still popular today?

Navajo Moccasins

Native American groups have made moccasins for thousands of years. These soft shoes are made from animal skins. Different groups make moccasins in different ways. Traditional Navajo moccasins were often made from deerskin and either reached the ankle or the knee.

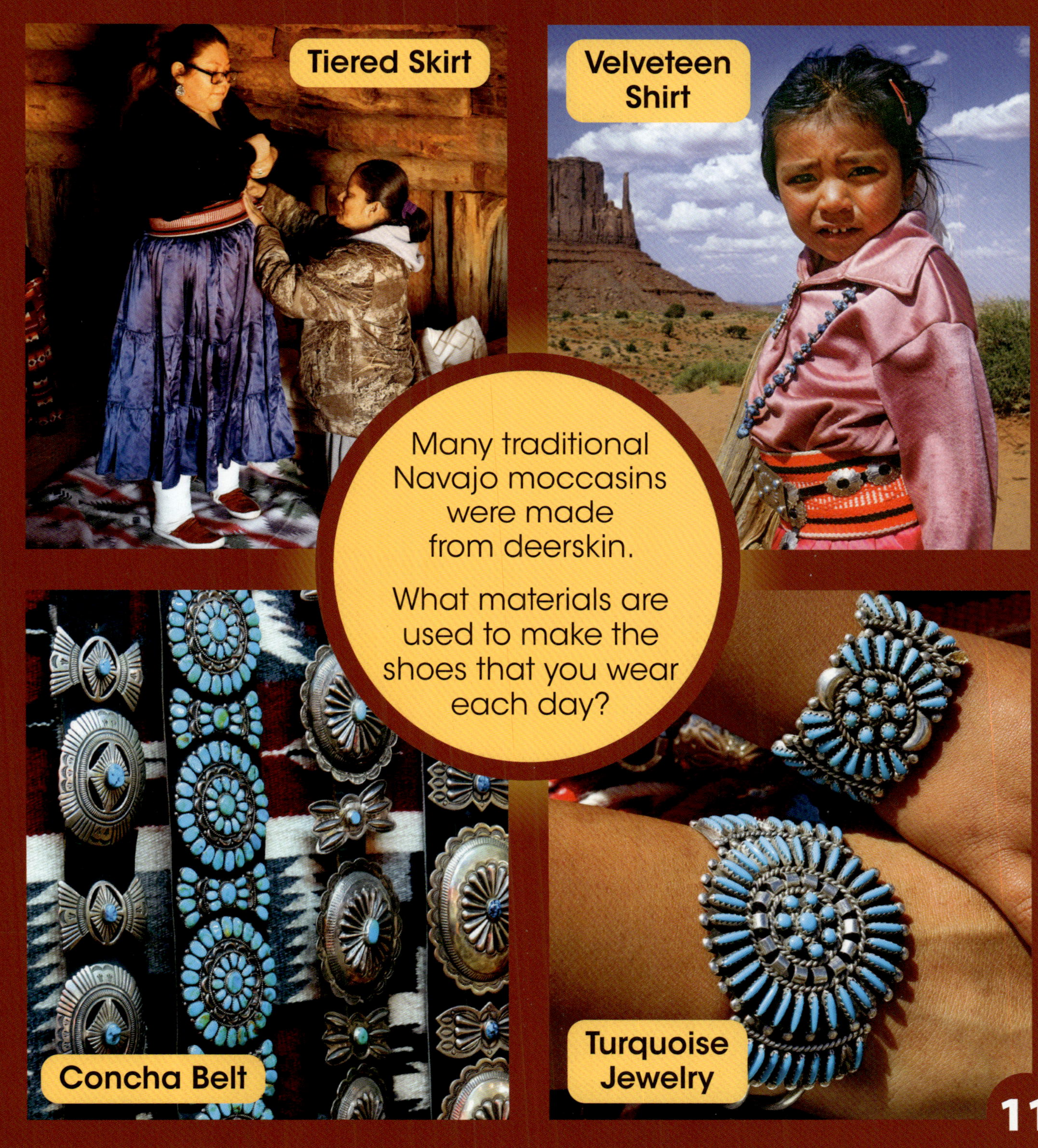

Many traditional Navajo moccasins were made from deerskin.

What materials are used to make the shoes that you wear each day?

Jewish Shawls

A tallit is a Jewish prayer shawl. It looks like a long, wide scarf. Tallits are often white with navy or black stripes across the ends. They have fringes called tzitzit at the edges. Many Jewish men wear a head covering. The yarmulke is the most common. It is also known as a kippah.

Kippah

Headscarf

The Jewish tallit is designed with fringes at the end.

Is any clothing that you wear similar to the tallit?

Tzitzit

Kittel

German Wools

Germans traditionally wore clothes made from spun wool. Their clothing often showed what sort of job they worked at. Lederhosen are short leather pants. Hosenträger are suspenders. They are often worn by German men and boys.

German women wear aprons as part of their traditional clothes.

When might you wear an apron?

French Embroidery

Many traditional French clothes are made from cotton, linen, silk, wool, and lace. The French use embroidery as a way to decorate clothing. Petit-point and chenille are embroidery stitches. Beads are strung on wire to make flowers. They are used as jewelry.

Dress

Beret

The French may wear traditional clothing to special events.

What do you wear on special occasions?

White Bonnet

Shoes

Irish Dance Wear

Irish dancers wear traditional clothes. Women wear peasant dresses. They are embroidered with special patterns. Dresses often are bright colors. Men wear pants or a kilt and a shirt. Some dancers wear a brat. A brat is a cloak that hangs from the shoulder.

Irish dancers wear special dance costumes.

What costumes do you wear to dance?

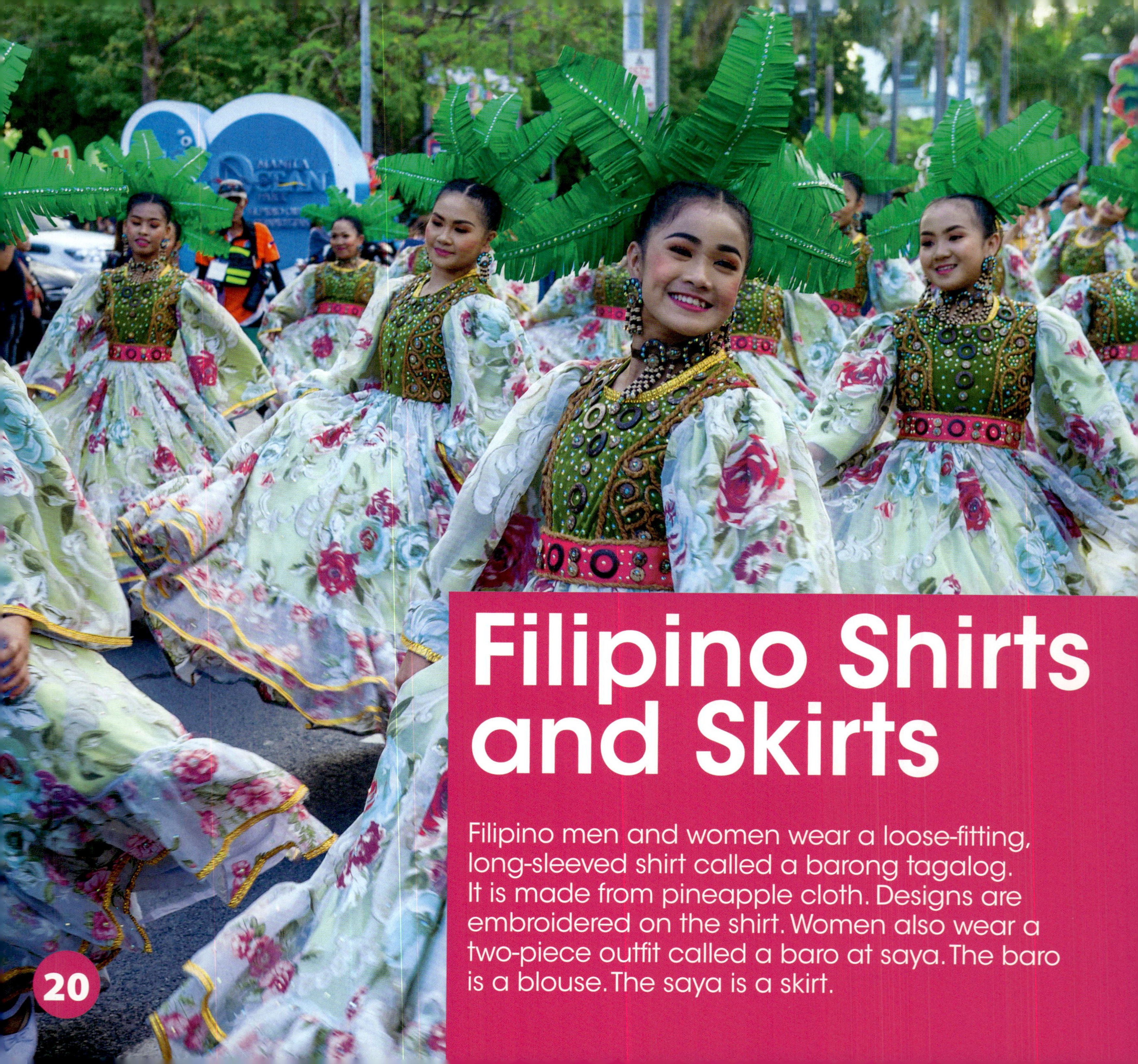

Filipino Shirts and Skirts

Filipino men and women wear a loose-fitting, long-sleeved shirt called a barong tagalog. It is made from pineapple cloth. Designs are embroidered on the shirt. Women also wear a two-piece outfit called a baro at saya. The baro is a blouse. The saya is a skirt.

Bahag

Barong

Some Filipinos traditionally wear headgear.

Do you wear anything like headgear?

Headgear

Saya

Matching Activity

You have learned about many kinds of clothing in the United States.

Match the name of each clothing item below to the correct picture.

Irish Dance Wear	Navajo Moccasins	Jewish Shawls
French Silks	Chinese Silk Robes	Filipino Shirts and Skirts
Ukrainian Linens	Mexican Poncho	German Wools

KEY WORDS

Research has shown that as much as 65 percent of all written material published in English is made up of 300 words. These 300 words cannot be taught using pictures or learned by sounding them out. They must be recognized by sight. This book contains 75 common sight words to help young readers improve their reading fluency and comprehension. This book also teaches young readers several important content words, such as proper nouns. These words are paired with pictures to aid in learning and improve understanding.

Page	Sight Words First Appearance
4	a, and, are, from, is, made, more, no, of, often, than, there, use, with, young
5	do, on, their, what, you
6	as, come, if, it, long, may, men, or, over, sometimes, that, the, they, well
7	kind, make, your
8	America, been, by, for, have, head, in, keep, many, people, years
9	but, old, still, think, very, why
10	animal, different, groups, these, ways, were
11	day, each
12	also, at, like, looks, most, white
13	any
15	an, might, part, when
18	some, this

Page	Content Words First Appearance
4	belt, clothing, embroidery, girls, linens, polotno, shirt, skirt, sorochka, Ukrainians, women
5	bast shoes, korsetka, ubka
6	hat, jacket, knees, ku, mao, pants, qun, robes, silk, tunics, yi fu
7	cheongsam, material, scarf, xie
8	Central America, cotton, coverings, Mexico, ponchos, South America, wool
9	design, huarache, rebozo, sombrero
10	ankle, moccasins, skins
11	jewelry
12	fringes, kippah, shawls, stripes, tallit, tzitzit, yarmulke
13	headscarf, kittel
14	boys, hosenträger, job, lederhosen, suspenders
15	aprons, dirndl, tracht
16	beads, chenille, flowers, lace, petit-point, wire
17	beret, bonnet, dress, events
18	brat, cloak, kilt, shoulder
19	brogues, cap, costumes, sweater
20	baro at saya, barong tagalog, outfit
21	bahag

Published by Lightbox Learning
276 5th Avenue, Suite 704 #917
New York, NY 10001
Website: www.openlightbox.com

Library of Congress Control Number available upon request.

ISBN 978-1-5105-5994-3 (hardcover)
ISBN 978-1-5105-5995-0 (multi-user eBook)

Printed in Guangzhou, China
1 2 3 4 5 6 7 8 9 0 25 24 23 22 21

092021
110820

Designer: Ana María Vidal Project Coordinator: John Willis

Every reasonable effort has been made to trace ownership and to obtain permission to reprint copyright material. The publisher would be pleased to have any errors or omissions brought to its attention so that they may be corrected in subsequent printings. The publisher acknowledges Alamy, Dreamstime, Getty Images, and Wikimedia as the primary image suppliers for this title.